affirmations & advice for girls

90 Days of Powerful Words

Affirmations & Advice for Girls

affirmations & advice for girls

90 Days of Powerful Words

Affirmations & Advice for Girls

by

Onedia N. Gage, Ph. D.

affirmations & advice for girls

library of congress

All Rights Reserved © 2017
Rev. Onedia N. Gage

No part of this of book may be reproduced or transmitted in
Any form or by any means, graphic, electronic, or mechanical,
Including photocopying, recording, taping, or by any
Information storage or retrieval system, without the
Permission in writing from the publisher.

Purple Ink, Inc. Press

For Information:
Purple Ink, Inc.
P O Box 300113
Houston, TX 77230

www.purpleink.net ♦ www.onediagagespeaks.com

publish@purpleink.net ♦ onediagage@onediagagespeaks.com

ISBN:

978-1-939119-66-7

Printed in United States

Other Books by
Onedia N. Gage, Ph. D.

Are You Ready for 9th Grade . . . Again? A Family's Guide to Success
As We Grow Together Daily Devotional for Expectant Couples
As We Grow Together Prayer Journal for Expectant Couples
As We Grow Together Bible Study: Her Workbook
As We Grow Together Bible Study: His Workbook
The Best 40 Days of My Life: A Journey of Spiritual Renewal
The Blue Print: Poetry for the Soul
From Fat to Fit in 90 Days: A Fitness Journal
From Two to One: The Notebook for the Christian Couple
Hannah's Voice: Powerful Lessons in Prayer
Her Story The Legacy of Her Fight: Bible Study
Her Story The Legacy of Her Fight: The Devotional
Her Story The Legacy of Her Fight: The Legacy Journal
Her Story The Legacy of Her Fight: Prayers and Journal
ILY! A Mother Daughter Relationship Workbook
In Her Own Words: Notebook for the Christian Woman
In Purple Ink: Poetry for the Spirit
Intensive Couples Retreat: Her Workbook
Intensive Couples Retreat: His Workbook
Living A Whole Life: Sermons Which Provide, Prompt, and Promote Life
Love Letters to God from a Teenage Girl
The Measure of a Woman: The Details of Her Soul
The Notebook: For Me, About Me, By Me
The Notebook for the Christian Teen
On This Journey Daily Devotional for Young People
On This Journey Prayer Journal for Young People
On This Journey Prayer Journal for Young People, Vol. 2

affirmations & advice for girls

One Day More Than We Deserve Prayer Journal for the Growing Christian
Promises, Promises: A Christian Novel
Queen in the Making: 30 Week Bible Study for Teen Girls
She Spoke Volumes . . . And Then Some
Six Months of Solitude: The Sanctity of Singleness Notebook
Tools for These Times: Timely Sermons for Uncertain Times
With An Anointed Voice: The Power of Prayer
Yielded and Submitted: A Woman's Journey for a Life Dedicated to God
Yielded and Submitted: A Woman's Journey for a Life Dedicated to God An Intimate Study
Yielded and Submitted: A Woman's Journey for a Life Dedicated to God Prayers and Journal

dedication

to the millions of girls who are searching for a better version of herself and who are trying to overcome the issues she has encountered

to the millions who do not believe in herself, does not love herself, and does not believe she can do either

to the millions of girls who need an upgrade of herself-esteem and self-worth

to the millions of girls who reject herself because she doubts her abilities, current, and the future

to the millions of girls who are hurting internally, mentality and emotionally

For ALL girls, You Have the POWER TO OVERCOME!

affirmations & advice for girls

scriptures

¹⁴ I praise you because I am fearfully and wonderfully made;
your works are wonderful,
I know that full well.

Psalm 139:14

³ Not only so, but we also glory in our sufferings, because we know that suffering produces perseverance; ⁴ perseverance, character; and character, hope. ⁵ And hope does not put us to shame, because God's love has been poured out into our hearts through the Holy Spirit, who has been given to us.

Romans 5:3-5

More Than Conquerors

³¹ What, then, shall we say in response to these things? If God is for us, who can be against us? ³² He who did not spare his own Son, but gave him up for us all—how will he not also, along with him, graciously give us all things? ³³ Who will bring any charge against those whom God has chosen? It is God who justifies. ³⁴ Who then is the one who condemns? No one. Christ Jesus who died—more than that, who was raised to life—is at the right hand of God and is also interceding for us. ³⁵ Who shall separate us from the love of Christ? Shall trouble or hardship or persecution or famine or nakedness or danger or sword? ³⁶ As it is written:

"For your sake we face death all day long;
  we are considered as sheep to be slaughtered."

[37] No, in all these things we are more than conquerors through him who loved us. [38] For I am convinced that neither death nor life, neither angels nor demons, neither the present nor the future, nor any powers,[39] neither height nor depth, nor anything else in all creation, will be able to separate us from the love of God that is in Christ Jesus our Lord.

Romans 8:31-39

28 Her children arise and call her blessed;
  her husband also, and he praises her:
29 "Many women do noble things,
  but you surpass them all."
30 Charm is deceptive, and beauty is fleeting;
  but a woman who fears the Lord is to be praised.
31 Honor her for all that her hands have done,
  and let her works bring her praise at the city gate.

Proverbs 31:28-31

Dear God:

Thank You Lord for making me a girl! For all of what I did not experience, thank You! I know that there were days that I complained about my personal situations and my personal misfortunes, by my own definition, but then You revealed to me that there are other girls who have experienced far worse than I ever have. For those complaints, I apologize.

Thank You so much for creating me and ordering my path so that I could arrive in some amazing places—none of which I ever imagined or planned for myself. I am thankful that I can impact girls in my daily life; the type of impact for which I am grateful.

Thank You for Ms. S. Douglas, Mrs. Thomas, Mrs. Allen, Mrs. Berry, Ms. Ashley Salley, Mrs. Lightfoot, Ms. Freeman, Mrs. Prothrow, Ms. McDaniel, Ms. Colbert, and the women who I have forgotten or never knew their names or their contribution according to Your will in my life. I want to be that woman to some girls who need to see what hope and love looks like and feels like. The women You sent me taught me so much and believed in the amazing that could happen to me and it did.

Finally, Lord, I pray that You keep the girls close to You so that they can reach Your will for their lives. Keep them encouraged. Help me reach more young ladies.

Thank You for choosing me! In Your Son, Jesus' name, I pray.

affirmations & advice for girls

90 Days of Powerful Words

table of contents

Dedication	9
Scriptures	11
Prayer	13
Letters	17
Poem: A Warrior Mentality	21
Instructions	23
Affirmations and Advice	25
A Final Word	129
Poem: Clear the Mechanism	131
Poem: Identity Crisis	133
Poem: The Nerve to Dream	135
Resources	137
Acknowledgements	139
About the Girl and Girl's Advocate	141

affirmations & advice for girls

Dear Girl:

I just know that you are in need of help. You are in trouble! You are being stalked and sought out at an alarming rate. Your self-esteem is really low. I want you to recover and enhance your self-esteem and your whole life.

You are a girl! You were chosen to be a girl! You are a powerful being. You also thrive on love, nurture and care. These elements are critical.

Get ready to transform. Prepare to change. Be ready to achieve at an all-time high! This is your time! You are capable and able to be a strong girl who grows up to be a strong woman. This is my investment in you and your future. I do not know your story and I do not know your future. I do know that you need help on this journey. Here is part of it.

I love you because I know that you are trying to survive your circumstances and situation. You are trying to make the best of events outside of your control.

I love you because you need it. You are so very hurt and angry, emotionally malnourished and broken. There are days that you want to quit. Somedays you want to quit more than once in that same day.

You are a girl. Your power is different. Your abilities are unique. I believe in you. I need you to believe in yourself. Over the next 100 days, I want you to change your mind about yourself. It is important that you embrace who you are and what you want for your life.

affirmations & advice for girls

You can overcome the events, which have hurt. From that boy or girl who hurt you to the family member who raped you, you can heal. Forgive. Love. Overcome. Achieve.

Be brave. Be bold. Be outrageous. Be outlandish. All on your own behalf.

I love you! I look forward to your journey!

Contact me anytime at onediagage@onediagagespeaks.com or @onediangage or 713.705.5530. I would love to hear about your journey!

Love in Purple,

Onedia N. Gage

90 Days of Powerful Words

Dear Advocate of the Girl:

You have a hard job. You are her advocate. Her cheerleader. You have survived her storms and her events. You are begging her to talk. I understand your struggle. This journey has been taxing at the very least.

Then you do it all again tomorrow. She is finding her way and she need a roadmap and the GPS. She needs you. I know that your job gets hard and sometimes you want to quit; sometimes several times in one day. The job is not negotiable but you already know that.

Continue to pour into her, especially when you do not see the evidence of your labor. She is listening. She may even hear you and eventually she will do what you say.

Ask questions. Answer her questions. Keep her honest. Teach her daily. Use this book to support your work. There is no replacement for the power of your voice and influence.

Keep yourself together. It is easy to forget about yourself while trying to keep her together with glue and glitter. Both of you will recover at some point. Until then, keep reading and keep her talking.

Let me know if you need anything. Feel free to contact me at onediagage@onediagagespeaks.com or @onediangage or 713.705.5530.

Love in Purple,

Onedia N. Gage

affirmations & advice for girls

A Warrior Mentality

By Onedia N. Gage, Ph. D.

Love like a warrior
Fight
Eat
All like a warrior

A steel trap—mind your mind
Sharp and strong
Read
Read
Read
Sharpen the mind
Write
Write
Write
Sleep
Eat well
Relax
All like a warrior

Warriors breed warriors
Warriors achieve
A warrior mentality succeeds
A warrior exceeds the minimum standards
Warriors fight
Warriors fight fair
Warriors wage war over injustices

Prepared warrior

affirmations & advice for girls

Strong warrior
Evident warrior
Caring warrior

Act like a warrior
A warrior attitude
A warrior behavior

A warrior mentality

Reprinted from <u>In Purple Ink: Poetry for the Spirit</u>

instructions for this affirmations and advice

- Read the affirmation out loud at least twice.

- Read the advice. Make notes. Ask questions.

- There is a reflection portion. Those lines should be used to makes notes on how the affirmation and the advice caused you to take action and how it made you feel.

- Take your time. Spend as much time as you need to on each affirmation.

- Expect to grow.

- Share only what you need to so that you can be successful.

affirmations & advice for girls

Affirmations & Advice For Girls

affirmations & advice for girls

Day 1

I am a girl.

I am a girl who is smart.

I am a girl who is pretty.

I am a girl who is kind.

I am a girl! It took me a long time to accept these statements as true about myself. When others noticed, I was not any more comfortable with the statements than I had been after I accepted them. After I was able to accept those statements as true, I was able to grow as a girl. Embrace the statements.

REFLECTION

_____

_____

_____

affirmations & advice for girls

Day 2

I am great.

I am dynamic.

_____

These are important and powerful words, which are true about you. These statements are true because there are some things that you do well. Whether it is art or music, singing or math, you have gifts and talents. You are good at something and maybe more than one. More importantly, you are important to someone and probably many some bodies. Do not discount your greatness. You are not a good judge of that.

REFLECTION

_____
_____

_____

90 Days of Powerful Words

Day 3

I am intelligent.

I am powerful.

_____

These are words will take awhile to embrace, especially if you cannot see evidence of it in your grades. Or what you perceive is your influence. You are smarter than you realize. You need to focus on more representative grades. Get help as needed. Power is about making good decisions and asking questions when you need help. Power is using your best self to get the best from you and those around you. Then doing more. Power is never giving up.

REFLECTION

_____
_____
_____

affirmations & advice for girls

Day 4

I will overcome the bad events, which have happened in my past.

Often, you respond to others based on the thought process that everyone knows your past when that is actually not true. The other fact is that everyone has a past with varying ranges of embarrassment and issues. The fact is that you can and WILL recover from this past and these bad events. You will recover to be stronger and more powerful because of the wisdom you have gained through that experience. You will be even stronger when you are able to share your past with others in order to help them to grow.

REFLECTION

_____
_____
_____

Day 5

I am motivated to do my best work every day. Today!

This is a matter of will. Sometimes we do not want to do what we are supposed to do, however, we cannot quit. We have to do our work every day. I know that being motivated is not easy, but it is easier than self-defeat and failure. I would rather that you do your best today because you do not feel like it, than not to do so and regret the consequences. You only get one today. You never know when today's work will turn into tomorrow's success. If we miss this opportunity, then we will never have it again. We cannot afford those days when we miss the opportunity because we did not feel like it.

REFLECTION

_____
_____
_____

affirmations & advice for girls

Day 6

I will exceed my own expectations today!

Take your life seriously so that others will do the same. This is a critical time for you to understand the investment of others in your life. I think we need to meet our own expectations. When we exceed our own expectations, we can definitely exceed others'. Other people cannot define that for you. You need to be intentional about what you will achieve each day. You need to make a list and set goals for the day. You need to set these expectations each day so that you can see progress in your life. This is not time to leave success to chance. We cannot cross our fingers and close our eyes, hoping that all will be well.

REFLECTION

_____

_____

_____

Day 7

I will focus on school and work expectations better than I did yesterday!

Protect your education and learning time at all times. It is too valuable to leave without guidance. This is the only time you will have to complete this educational opportunity at this time in your life. Once this time has passed, there is not another opportunity to repeat this work or recapture this time. You will not know that you need it until you do not have it.

REFLECTION

_____

_____

_____

Day 8

I love me!

I love myself!

I know that this is hard but it is possible. You can do it. You can do it regardless of why you currently don't love yourself. You first have to forgive yourself. This is the hardest part. You have consider yourself forgivable. You DO deserve your own forgiveness. I know you messed up and made a mistake. You are worthy of forgiveness. 'But you do not know what I did.' While that is true, you are forgiven. Go make it right. Whatever went wrong, go make it right. This is the time when you renew yourself and consider yourself a creature worthy of love.

REFLECTION

Day 9

I love me just as I am!

I love me even though I should not and especially when others do not.

Others will be critical of you. Do not add to that activity. You deserve love. You deserve to love yourself and the benefits of that love. You should stop being critical of yourself. Stop allowing others to do the same. This is a growing time for you. This is not a time to become so critical of yourself that you have difficulties with looking at yourself, believing in yourself, and or trying to accomplish your dreams or even just being successful in your daily life, such as school requirements, and social interactions. Love and believe.

REFLECTION

_____

_____

_____

affirmations & advice for girls

Day 10

I will overcome adversity with grace, poise, and love.

The only person who can stop you from being great is you. Adversity will happen. Adversity is not personal. It is part of what builds character, builds perseverance and forms your ability to overcome events and people, which want to cause you to fail. The grace, which you need, will come from understanding how to see the good in the adversity. Poise is being able to handle the bad with an image, which others will admire and respect, and mostly they will be surprised at how well you handled it. Love is the key, which is often omitted. The world does not expect love, rather expects revenge. Love your enemies in a manner, which lets them know that their actions leave you untouched.

REFLECTION

Day 11

I will look at myself and my features without criticism.

Learn to look at yourself in the mirror without criticism. I am clear that you have to check your image. Make those investigations with some praise more often than you criticize yourself. Further, consider the origin of the standards by which you are criticizing yourself. Models in magazines have makeup teams. They do not look like that naturally. All of that is done the day of that photo shoot. Ask yourself does 'perfect' hair and eyebrows make you the person you are. Are you any less intelligent or determined, lovable or enthusiastic without perfect nails? Because the answer is no, spend time on what matters: is your heart healthy? Is your mind at capacity? Spend time on those areas which make you great.

REFLECTION

_____

_____

_____

affirmations & advice for girls

Day 12

I am fearless!

Fear is a paralyzing emotion! Fear stops good people from being great. Fearful is a terrible place to be and often about nothing. Fear should be dismissed. Easier said than done? I know. Trying everything you desire is greater than being scared to do so. Working to be first in your class is worth it. Fear would have you to stop. If the outcome is going to be better than not trying, DO IT! Try it with all that you are! Do it! Do not let your fear or someone else's fear cause you to miss something, which could be great for you! I live by the following: Do it Big! Do it Now! Do it Afraid!

Be fearless! It is will usher greatness into your life.

REFLECTION

_____

_____

_____

Day 13

I am a conqueror!

Conqueror is defined as a person who is a winner, victorious, overcomer, achiever, and master with force and effort. This is critical for our success. In order to obtain certain levels of accomplishment and achievement, you may have to use force and make a lot of effort. This is the requirement to be a conqueror. Conquerors are respected and we are watched and admired. We however are just trying to survive our circumstances. We need to be a conqueror to do so. Do not stand by and watch your life. Step up and stand up so that you can participate in your future and your victorious outcome. Be a conqueror. It does require work but well worth it.

REFLECTION

Day 14

Victory belongs to me!

Victory may look distant, but use doubt and bleakness to fuel your actions. The jealousy of others should have no bearing on what you do. You have what you dream of and what you want. You will see many events and many injustices in your life. Take note and take heart to overcome those with the vision of victory in your mind and your heart. You are victorious. You are victorious because you chose to be. This is a choice. Some people choose to do nothing. Others choose to win. We choose to win by doing the work, which is required and the effort that is necessary. This is not going to be easy. I want you to understand that. This is your life, so you can't expect anyone to work harder for it than you. Victory is imminent. Victory!

REFLECTION

Day 15

I will be positive with others today even when I do not feel like it.

Negativity requires energy we need to use on other aspects of our lives. Being positive also keeps negative away from you. You cannot entertain the negative if you are being positive. This means that you cannot entertain the gossip and the negative forecasts for your life. Negativity is the opportunity people use to get you away from your goal. Do not give in. It is a cooperative effort. When the gossip starts or the negativity commences, change the subject. Ask them what they are working on in their lives or did they do the homework? This changes the focus and the tone of the conversation. Either they will participate or go away.

REFLECTION

_____

_____

_____

affirmations & advice for girls

Day 16

I am not defined by my past even if it was yesterday.

_____

You are going to make some mistakes, but do not quit and do not let those mistakes define you. This is not a suggestion. Do NOT let it happen. There was a young lady who was crowned the first African American Miss America. Very big deal. She made a mistake with some photos. She could have let that bury her, but she did not. She went on to become a great musician, actor and community activist. She made a mistake. She could have quit. She could have let others chase her away from her dreams. The only person who can define you is you. Do not let those mistakes take away your spirit and your drive, your determination and your will. People will want to remind you of your past. Let them. Then move on with your life!

REFLECTION

_____
_____
_____

Day 17

I am not defined by how much money my family has.

_____

Money has a place but it does not define who you are or what you will achieve or accomplish. This has be rejected immediately. This could be discouraging if your family is considered poor. This is also discouraging if your family has money and it dictates your life's course and the path you have for yourself is not aligned. This is the time to make your life out of 'nothing.' Enough people have this success story. They 'come from nothing.' They 'come from humble beginnings.' This translates into we did not have very much money and other socioeconomic disadvantages. Do not let this stop you from being your best. Money is not the last word on your life. It is helpful but it is not the last word.

REFLECTION

_____
_____
_____

affirmations & advice for girls

Day 18

I am not defined by where I live.

Look for love in your situation. Whether you live in a 'shack' or a 'mansion,' who you are is only a proud product if you have achieved your goals and accomplished your dreams. This is independent of the people with whom you live. I have learned in my life that I can set the tone and raise the bar for others by being myself. This means that I do not consider my beginnings when I step out to achieve my dreams and goals. I want to help others to achieve their dreams and goals. I encourage you to ignore the surroundings, which do not urge you to be your best. I am hopeful that you will overcome that guilt that comes with success in the presence of others who have not achieved what they desired.

REFLECTION

_____

_____

_____

Day 19

I am not defined by what I see.

Statistically, some girls are not supposed to live to reach the age of 18. Those who do reach age 18, are projected to have a baby before graduating. Some will not graduate. Some of those will have attempted suicide. Others are destined to use drugs, drink alcohol, and smoke cigarettes. There is a chance of sex trafficking. Prostitution. There are 100 issues, which could keep you from being great. Do not be one of that 100. Do not let what you see or do not see define you. If you are the first to graduate, then great! Set a new trend. Create a new legacy. Define yourself. Defy the statistics. Challenge the odds.

REFLECTION

_____
_____
_____

Day 20

I can learn.

I will learn.

I am learning.

Your education matters because it offer you choice for your future. The chances that people give to people without high school diplomas and college degrees are minimal. Without those academic designations, you are not considered smart and may be marginalized or discounted or discarded because of an undervaluation of your worth. Do not stand in your own way. Actively participate in your education.

REFLECTION

_____

_____

_____

Day 21

I will succeed, even when other believe otherwise.

Don't accept negative projections in your life. Believe in yourself, especially when nobody else does. Sometimes, you will be the only person who believes and understands your vision for your life. Do not abandon those beliefs under any circumstances. Success is dependent on you and you alone. Cast away the negative so that the positive can be seen, felt and heard. You will need to repeat this to yourself daily. You will need to remember this when you want to quit. Be bold enough to take a chance on yourself.

REFLECTION

_____
_____
_____

Day 22

I am beautiful.

You are beautiful. Your beauty does not take away the beauty of another and likewise, another person does not away from your beauty. You can be beautiful without makeup and without consistent alterations and adjustments to your person. Remember that when you admire those musicians and celebrities, they have the benefit of a team of personal stylists who do all of that immediately before the shoot. Further, if they magazine editor does not like something, there is always Photoshop and airbrush. Be okay with you are in regards to how you look. No excuses. No judgment.

REFLECTION

_____

_____

_____

Day 23

I am better than good enough!

_____

That is such a powerful statement. This is a statement, which requires focus. And confidence. And fearlessness. You will encounter some negative people; they may live with you, they may have birthed you. However, you have control over whether their words have power or not. Their words only have power if you allow that to be the case. So discard the negative. Their love for you cannot co-exist with their rejection of you and your dreams. Only listen to what is powerful and constructive. You are better than good enough. You are great!

REFLECTION

affirmations & advice for girls

Day 24

I am excited to learn.

Being smart is a decision. Being smart is okay. Being smart does not cause you to judge others. Being smart does not cause others to judge you. You do not have to be ashamed to be smart or to want to be smart. Do not be apologetic for being smart or wanting to be smart. Be excited to invest in yourself, inclusive of learning. This is a great place to be. You are ready to compete in the world with that level of excitement. You will not be easily deterred with that enthusiasm. This is a great time in your life. Set high goals for where that excitement can lead you.

REFLECTION

Day 25

I am only at risk to succeed.

Based on many factors, some known, others unknown, some children are labeled 'at risk.' When I first learned of this designation, I was confused. This designation is based on statistics developed by educators. This made me question their credentials. You may be labeled at risk, however that is not at risk to fail unless you want to fail. You are only at risk to succeed. If you access all that is available to you, which others use to succeed, you will succeed. Defy the labels! Defy the odds. Define your path—with all of the landmines and obstacles. With everyone looking, be the success no one thinks you can be, based on the issues you do not control.

REFLECTION

Day 26

My chances of failure do not determine my future or my success.

Intrinsic motivation is what is missing from children you succeed and children who do not. Vision may be lacking from those who do and those who do not. These are learned behaviors. You can learn to develop vision and use that vision to succeed. You can develop internal motivation so that you can be hungry enough to want to succeed. You only fail because you did not try, you did not want to succeed, or you lacked the resources. This may require a little extra planning. We will eliminate the chances for failure by planning, trying, and being hungry enough to go after what we want.

REFLECTION

_____

_____

_____

Day 27

I am dynamic student!

Do not make excuses for who you are. Be that dynamic student. She asks questions in class. She does all of her homework, turns it in on time, and informs the teacher when there was an unresolved struggle while doing the homework. This is a dynamic student. She studies. She sets the achievement bar high. She does not become discouraged, but if she does, then she seeks help from a counselor, teacher, or trusted advocate. She goes to college. She tries her best at all levels. She does not quit.

REFLECTION

affirmations & advice for girls

Day 28

I am excited to be myself.

_____

I know that this can be tough. Find the positive details about yourself. There are at least 75 great things about you. So be excited about you. Do not make excuses for you are. Nor should you apologize for being who you are. Be you. Be comfortable in your body and who you represent. This is giant task but you can do it.

REFLECTION

_____
_____
_____

90 Days of Powerful Words

Day 29

I will achieve my dreams!

Pursue your dreams regardless of what others say about them. These are your dreams. The only persons whose opinion matters about them is yours. You will face obstacles and hardships in the pursuit of those dreams. We must build character and perseverance in this journey. Work toward your dreams daily. Every day you will be closer than you were the day before. This is a daily pursuit of excellence, which leads others to do the same. Some of the most respected inventors and entrepreneurs were convinced at some point to quit because of their lack of immediate success but they persisted. We have great items because they didn't quit.

REFLECTION

_____

_____

_____

affirmations & advice for girls

Day 30

I will overcome my fears!

___

I want you to try everything that makes scared to death! It is there where your best work will be done. I know that this is not your ideal scenario, however this is one way to overcome your fears. I am afraid every time I publish a book or approach a podium. However, I am going to keep publishing and speaking because that is what I am designed to do. I want you to try even while you are afraid. Use your fear to fuel your success. While this may be easier said than done, I want you to try in spite of your fear.

REFLECTION

___

___

___

Day 31

I am an overcomer.

I can overcome the issues that I encounter.

I am an overcomer! I am still overcoming daily. I put one foot in front of the other even when I do not have the answers I would like to have in order to reach the place I would like to reach. I have goals too and I want to achieve them all. I take my days one at a time. I address my projects one at a time. I complete them and then I start the next. This life will try to intimidate you and discourage you from trying and succeeding, however, please just stay focused on what is before you so that you can be successful in overcoming that obstacle and landmine. You can do it. You are an overcomer!

REFLECTION

_____

_____

_____

affirmations & advice for girls

Day 32

I have a beautiful spirit.

I am beautiful inside and out.

Be yourself! Do not try to please others by being someone that you are not. This is a dangerous place to operate. You are an awesome person. Your spirit—your inner being—is beautiful. No one can change the nature of your being. You are a powerful young lady with a bright future. It is permissible and expected for you to be kind, helpful, compassionate, and loving, especially to strangers. Even when others are not kind or helpful, compassionate or loving, you be those aspects. You have a beautiful spirit. Share it with others.

REFLECTION

_____

_____

_____

Day 33

I am a game changer.

_____

I am a game changer! Those are some powerful words. The definition of game changer according to dictionary.com is
a person or thing that dramatically changes the course, strategy, character, etc., of something. This is you! What are you going to change in this world by being the person you are designed to be? Someone is waiting on your medical breakthrough or your mathematical procedure or your innovative discovery. You cannot stop working toward it—no matter what. Be brave enough to change the game! Be a leader! Be an innovator! Be You!

REFLECTION

_____
_____

_____

affirmations & advice for girls

Day 34

The best I have to offer, I will offer it today so that I can be my best self.

I will give my best today!

I will give my best today! Give yourself every day. You cannot afford to take a break. Achievement is a daily activity. You won't achieve it all in one day. So you have to work toward it every day. So you are to do your best daily. You can never do poor work or quit from your work. There are no excuses for poor performance. I think that we discount ourselves and think our best is not good enough. Your best is great!

REFLECTION

_____

_____

_____

Day 35

I am positive.

_____

Positive is the best way to approach and be. It is harder to be positive than to be negative, however it is better than to be positive. Optimism is an understated quality, which has high value. Optimism is defined as reflecting a favorable view of events and conditions and the expectations of a positive outcome. This requires focus. What is the silver-lining behind this set back? What is the delay teaching me? These are two of the questions that lead to understanding the concept of optimism and positivity. Your being positive should be the frame to your life. This is lifelong experience. Be positive.

REFLECTION

_____
_____
_____

Day 36

I am energetic.

I am enthusiastic.

_____

Energy is required to be great. Enthusiastic is also required to be an achiever. These two qualities are noble. They are both rare as well. Energy is contagious, meaning that others around you will become energetic because of your energy. This is similar to the positive contagion. Enthusiasm is a contagious quality as well. The enthusiasm will ignite excitement. Your body language will communicate both of these. These two qualities will cause others to pay attention and change for the better.

REFLECTION

_____

_____

_____

Day 37

I listen to those who teach me.

I listen to those who advise me.

I listen to those who discipline me.

Find an advocate or mentor so that you can gain knowledge and wisdom about education, life and avoiding the need for discipline. This is critical for your success. When I have child in 'trouble,' I ask the child do you have a favorite teacher. Sometimes the answer is no, this is when I am afraid for the child. With an advocate, I can take the child to that person with whom the child already has a relationship and thus can hear the person, no matter what they are saying. The advocate assists in the success of the student. You need a cheerleader.

REFLECTION

_____

_____

_____

affirmations & advice for girls

Day 38

I promise to resist rejecting those who try to love me.

I will try to accept those who invest in me.

Everyone is not against you. You find it hard to trust adults. Someone important may have left you and you blame yourself for their departure. Maybe they made a promise, which they have faltered on. This is not what everyone else will do. Please try to trust those who seek to help you. If you want to understand why the person is trying to help, then ask respectfully. There are adults, which are sent to help you with making progress in your life, who are not going to leave or disappoint you. Trust. They are invested. Let them do so.

REFLECTION

_____

_____

_____

Day 39

I am worth loving.

I am worthy of being loved.

I apologize for every time love has cost you something it should not have cost you. As a young girl, your life should be drama-free and issue-free. Many cases this is not the case. I apologize. I know that I am not to blame or the cause, however no one has apologized yet, so let me be the first and maybe the only one who does so. "I am worthy of being loved without conditions or strings attached. I am worth loving without the costs others want to impose." The stories I hear are heartbreaking. You are worth love!

REFLECTION

_____

_____

_____

affirmations & advice for girls

Day 40

I am worth others trusting me.

You are trustworthy. Tell the truth. No matter what the consequence. All of the time. Keep your word and promises. Keep focus on what matters for you. You are trustworthy if you choose to be. Be where you are supposed to be at all times. Complete your work. Be on time to class. Go to every class. Follow directions. Follow your leadership. Ask for clarity when you do not understand. This is the way to become trustworthy. This is key for life.

REFLECTION

_____

_____

_____

Day 41

I trust myself.

———————————

Trusting yourself is an interesting accomplishment. It starts with belief. The belief that you are able to do that which you think and dream. This is the start of amazing: trust yourself. Trust starts with belief. If you can believe, then you can trust. What do you want to trust yourself to do? The only way is not fail yourself. Try. Try. Fail. Try again. Trusting yourself is being doing this daily and without a break. Trust yourself to be successful.

REFLECTION

———————————————————
———————————————————

———————————————————

Day 42

I trust myself to achieve.

You can achieve all of what you set your mind to and nothing for which you offer no effort. You have to give effort for the level of achievement you desire and deserve. You have to trust yourself to achieve. You have to want to achieve. At the highest possible level. What is stopping you from achieving the goals you have for yourself? This is in need of change. Achievement and accomplishment are a necessary measure for continuing to achieve. Once you achieve, then you will always want to achieve. Go for it—All out!!!

REFLECTION

_____

_____

_____

Day 43

I am worth believing in.

You are! You are worthy of the belief of others! You are also worthy of believing in yourself! You cannot expect others to believe in you if you do not believe in yourself. Why don't you believe in yourself? What happened which caused you not to believe in yourself? I hope that it was not because someone told you that you would not achieve anything. Please report those persons if you anyone says or has said that you would not be anything less than great. You are capable of everything that you can dream up and anything you see someone else do. Belief is possible! It starts with you!

REFLECTION

_____

_____

_____

Day 44

I am being groomed for greatness.

Every day that you attend school, read, complete projects, and learn new things in class or anywhere, you are being groomed for greatness. You are being trained for greatness. You are building the skills and knowledge for your future—your greatness. You are building work ethic. That work ethic will carry you very far. "Nothing beats a failure but a try" means that you cannot achieve anything without trying or doing something. You will be amazed at how many people quit right before achieving amazing things. Do not be that person. Greatness outlasts others. This work ethic separates you from those who will quit before success is realized.

REFLECTION

_____

_____

_____

Day 45

I am focused.

I am not going to get distracted about achieving my goals. I am focused. Repeat those words regularly. You need to be reminded. Please do not sabotage yourself by getting off track. Please do not sabotage your work by settling for less than your best. Stay focused. Stay focused and do not get distracted. Staying focused means that you cannot stop working on your projects, working toward the completion of your goals and dreams, and spending time getting better at your craft. Do not let anyone or anything deter you from your desires and dreams.

REFLECTION

---

affirmations & advice for girls

Day 46

I am focused on positive results from my positive actions and behaviors.

Without focus, we would not have the cellular phone, lights, televisions, cars, clothes, or anything else. I am certain that you will make a powerful contribution to this world if only you will stay focused and let no one and nothing stop you from arriving at your goal and accomplishing your wildest dreams. You are growing up in a time, which you have the world at your fingertips so it would appear that achievement should be easier. Pursue your dreams and goals with all that you are and all that you have. Give it your very best and then some!

REFLECTION

_____

_____

_____

Day 47

I am creative.

What do you think about? What do you want to achieve? What do you write? What problems do you solve? What consumes you? What do you draw? What excites you? What do you daydream about? You are a creative person. You are creative. You should be proud of that gift. You need embrace. You are creative! Do not others make you feel bad about it or tease you or discount yourself. Be determined to make that the best thing about you!

REFLECTION

_____
_____
_____

Day 48

I have a healthy mind.

I will enhance the health of my mind by reading and resting.

A healthy mind starts with a healthy diet. Drinking water. Exercise. Sleep. Resting. Reading and learning fuels a healthy mind. This stimulation will translate into the rest of your life. Take care of your mind. Guard what goes into your mind, including doubt, fear, and hopelessness. Reading affords power through knowledge and investigation. A healthy mind is important and keeping it healthy is important as well. Read. Read. Read.

REFLECTION

_____

_____

_____

Day 49

I have a healthy and open heart.

I will love freely.

I know that this will take some work. Your heart is healthy but it is guarded. It is not open because it has been hurt, damaged, and bruised; nearly broken. It can heal. It is repairable. Learning to forgive is the first step for the healthy and open heart of which I write. Also, loving freely is possible after forgiveness. Give new people a chance who actually try to invest in you and your life without it costing you things, which are damaging or harmful to you. Love those people who love you. Freely. Open and healthy heart!

REFLECTION

_____

_____

_____

affirmations & advice for girls

Day 50

I am healing from the issues, events and people, which have hurt me.

Your healing is imminent. Part of that happens with forgiveness. Forgiveness needs to happen. Start with yourself. You have been blaming yourself this entire time and now you need to stop blaming yourself. None of what has happened has been your fault. You did not hurt yourself. You did not leave yourself. You did not contribute to those situations and issues. Forgive yourself. Forgive them. Move forward with a healthy life ahead. Forgiveness guarantees your healing. Forgiveness frees you from the guilt and admonishment you have survived this entire time.

REFLECTION

_____

_____

_____

Day 51

I am productive.

I am a producer.

You were born to produce, to create, to perform, to contribute, to participate, and to dream. You are expected to those things at a high level. You are gifted to do something and you are expected to use those gifts to better the world. You are the next everything. The next teacher, doctor, inventor, entrepreneur, actor, singer, human resource manager, judge, attorney, engineer, and everything else! You are it! It might serve you well to do what you love, enjoy and what you are gifted to do. Produce!

REFLECTION

_____

_____

_____

affirmations & advice for girls

Day 52

I am a finisher!

I will complete the tasks before me.

I will complete the path of dreams.

I am very disturbed when I do not finish something I start. This is very rare for me. I usually finish after some time has passed. I believe that you should finish what you start. Anything worth starting is certainly worth finishing. Finish. No matter how long it takes or how much time has elapsed. Do not be discouraged because of the time that may have lapsed. Just restart where you left off. Ask for some help if it becomes difficult. Just finish. You will feel so much better if you finish.

REFLECTION

_____

_____

_____

Day 53

I have a loving soul.

Your soul is where your spirit rests. Your spirit needs nourishing. Your soul is free to be loving once you forgive yourself and others. Your soul is behind a high wall, which is understandable. However, what are you missing by not sharing that loving soul with others who are investing and invested in you and your future. That loving soul also will be able to love again and once it is nourished with people who love you and invest in you, you will have a loving soul and a nourished spirit. This renewed soul will flourish and grow.

REFLECTION

---

affirmations & advice for girls

Day 54

I will see the good in others.

I will see the good intentions of others.

———————————————

Seeing the good in others is a gift and this is coupled with the optimism we spoke of earlier. There is good in others just like there is good in you. See that good in others and give the benefit of the doubt. The intentions of others need to be examined for their worth. Every person is not after you, or to hurt you. See the great in others! Let them see the great in you!

REFLECTION

———————————————————
———————————————————
———————————————————

Day 55

I see the good in myself.

I am a good person. I see the good in myself. I can see the good in myself. These are possibly hard words to use and visualize and internalize, however, they become easier once you forgive, achieve, and love. When you forgive yourself, you will overcome the bad opinion of yourself. When you achieve, you will dismiss the low self-esteem. When you love, you can be free to return to seeing the good in yourself. When you feel better about yourself, others can see the same. Give yourself the benefit of the doubt. Give yourself a chance to become your best self. See the good in yourself. You are worth it.

REFLECTION

_____

_____

_____

affirmations & advice for girls

Day 56

I see the power in myself that others see in me.

When I tell you that you are powerful, you do not believe me. I understand that you have no reason to believe me. I do not know you and you do not know me. The problem is that I know thousands of people who are in a similar situation. The solution is to start here. I see power within you. Now it is your job to see within yourself. What do want for yourself? How badly do you want it? Go for it! That is the power that I am referring to. See your potential to be great. Avoid those who do not see that power and potential. Please stop the negative self-talk. Power!

REFLECTION

_____

_____

_____

Day 57

I see the potential in myself that others see in me.

———————————

This is hard to see but so very real. You have the potential to achieve all that you set out to achieve. This is the reason to exist: to achieve all that you can think of. This is your chance to understand what they see. Ask. When a teacher or parent says that they see potential in you, ask them what they mean. Ask them to be specific and to share how to reach that potential. Ask them to help you to reach that potential. One way to visualize your potential is to visit your dream job and take a picture there, even wearing the normal uniform. So if you want to be a pharmacist, try on the lab coat and take a photo. This visualization helps keep you focus.

REFLECTION

———————————
———————————
———————————

affirmations & advice for girls

Day 58

I will overcome my past with intention and purpose.

I do not know what your past holds, however the first question is are you alive. You are alive. The second question is can you continue with life. Yes, you should be able to move ahead. Whatever has happened in your past has made you stronger because of it. Use that bleak and sordid past to live a great life. Several successful people have horrible pasts. This has not stopped them from being successful. This intention and purpose will develop because of your past and your ability to overcome and not let your past take over your life. You have to live with intention and purpose. Overcomer!

REFLECTION

_____

_____

_____

Day 59

I will live my life with purpose.

Your purpose will define you. Purpose is defined as the reason someone exists. Your purpose will drive your decisions and your activities. You will pursue those activities, which fuel and support your purpose. Live for those activities. Give that purpose all of your energy and all of your time. When you are living and breathing your purpose, your life will be full, lacking nothing and serving others. What does that look like for you? What does your life's purpose? Who helps you with discovering your purpose? What will it take it for you to discover your purpose?

REFLECTION

_____

_____

_____

affirmations & advice for girls

Day 60

I will live my life with intentionality!

_____

Do not engage in activity, which does not support your purpose. Not many words left after that. Intentionally. Live your life dedicated and committed to your purpose. This intention will lead your steps and activities. Do not get sidetracked with other activities—ones which do not align with your purpose, your dreams, your goals, and your life. Learn to say no now so that you will not lose that focus later in life.

REFLECTION

_____
_____
_____

Day 61

I will live my life with love.

Hate is the opposite of love as reported by dictionary.com. I consider the opposite of love as indifference. Hate is what you may be using to live life right now. Or maybe disgust or dislike or disdain. But you are not living life with love. Your behavior suggests that you do not feel loved, you do not feel loving, nor do you feel like loving others. You reject the love of others even if they do not deserve that rejection. Love is easy to accept when you are not thriving on hate. Discard the hate. Yes, just throw it away. Leave it in the trashcan. Try love for a while, 10 days to be specific. If you can still remember to hate after those 10 days then you can continue to live in hate. But if you can love and be loved, then never hate again.

REFLECTION

_____

_____

_____

Day 62

I will live my life with exuberance and commitment.

Exuberance is defined as extremely joyful, enthusiastically and vigorous. Commitment is being tirelessly involved and dedicated to a situation or cause. You have to enthusiastically and joyfully and vigorously live your life. You live this life and you should do it with exuberance. You cannot quit on yourself, which is why commitment is important. This is a pair, which cannot be separated. Success will be easier when you can enjoy and stay the course. This may be a new concept to you, however it is necessary for you to understand and embrace. This will enhance your life.

REFLECTION

_____

_____

_____

Day 63

I am the making of a legacy.

Legacy is anything handed down from the past. You are creating a legacy for your children. You are possibly changing the legacy of your parents. Whichever is the case, you are the making of a legacy. You have the opportunity to change the legacy of your parents and you have a chance to overcome the horrible statistically bleak life, which the world hopes you will adopt to something overwhelmingly positive and against all statistical odds. Be the legacy of positive change and of hope which exists inside of your such that you can show others and help them to do the same. Legacy creates hope.

REFLECTION

---

affirmations & advice for girls

Day 64

I am the key to my future.

I speak to thousands of people each year. My most repeated advice is 'get out of your own way.' The only person who can truly stop you from being great is YOU! There are reasons to fail and to quit. Please do not be the reason. Persist with all that you are for the life of your dreams. You are the key factor in your future. Nothing can happen unless you do something.

REFLECTION

_____

_____

_____

Day 65

Failure is not an option!

Failure is not an option for me and my future!

Do not submit to failure. No matter what. Do not let your situation dictate your future. This is a matter of choice of positive people. You will decide whether you fail or not based on your behavior. You are the determining factor. No one makes that decision for you. Not even those who have said or disbelieved in your abilities. Decide to succeed, achieve and accomplish all that you set out to do so that you can be your best self!

REFLECTION

_____

_____

_____

affirmations & advice for girls

Day 66

I have a strong work ethic!

I will make it stronger through continuing to work hard.

Often the difference between two people is the work ethic. The one who reaches the finish line has work ethic. The one who reaches finish line has a no excuse policy. This is the difference. I have seen many talented people never reach their goal because of low work ethic. Conversely, I have seen mediocre talent reach great heights because of work ethic. Are you willing and able to work hard, consistently? That is the finisher of the race. That is what success looks like.

REFLECTION

_____

_____

_____

Day 67

I have extraordinary mental toughness, which helps me to accomplish all that is presented to me.

When I coach basketball, I teach the players to avoid listening to the other team's jeering. You have to be able to block out the noise of your perceived competition. In the movie, 'For Love of the Game,' the main character clears his head by saying, 'Clear the mechanism.' With that phrase, he stopped all of the noise in the crowd and was able to concentrate and focus so that he could play his best game. I invite you to do the same! Clear the mechanism. Exercise the mental toughness you have, which has been key to your life so far.

REFLECTION

_____
_____
_____

affirmations & advice for girls

Day 68

I will look at myself in the mirror without judgement or criticism.

I know that this is hard to do. It is too easy to think about the size of your lips or your forehead. Considering the fact that you have no control over your face, stop worrying about those features. Look into the mirror considering how to make your first speech. Or your first interview. Stop criticizing yourself so that you can see the beauty and the spectacular, which is evident to the rest of the world. I give you permission to like yourself, love yourself and be comfortable being yourself.

REFLECTION

_____

_____

_____

Day 69

I will heal from those areas that hurt me.

Your heart may hurt. Your soul may hurt. Your mind may hurt. Your spirit may hurt. They can also heal. Time will heal all wounds. Further, love can heal those places. Success will heal and remedy those areas, which ail you. Achievement will assist in your recovery. Do not let those hurts keep you from becoming successful. This hurt will not last always. Forgiveness also will expedite your healing. Forgive those who have hurt you. Take a deep breath and let it go. I know that this will not be easy. But your healing is worth it.

REFLECTION

---

affirmations & advice for girls

Day 70

I will not hurt others because I was hurt, even if they are the persons who hurt me.

There is a statement: 'Hurt people hurt people.' This means that people who are hurt, hurt other people. It also implies that they do it on purpose. When you do not return that hurt, they are surprised. Part of your healing is to avoid revenge, which would be easily a response to the hurt you have experienced. You cannot solve your hurt by hurting others, even if they hurt you first. Forgive. Love. Heal. Thrive. Succeed. Work. Achieve. Accomplish.

REFLECTION

Day 71

I have the power to create the life I want.

Intrinsic motivation is defined as built-in, hardwired, and natural motivation. This exists within most people, however it may be harder to access or witness than within others. This built-in motivation fuels the power within you. This motivation turns on the power so that achievement can take place. This power is necessary to create the life you want. This power is necessary to create the legacy that your life is destined to produce. The power is inside and it is accessible to you at all times.

REFLECTION

---

affirmations & advice for girls

Day 72

I can have the ideas I think and the dreams I dream.

I did not realize that people really do not believe in themselves until I understood that had no encouragement. They had discounted themselves so regularly and for so long that anything different was hard to believe. Dream BIG! No one should laugh at your dreams. No one should act like they are impossible. Do not let them discount those dreams. And neither should you! Have confidence and faith in your ideas and dreams. Avoid people who do not share your attitude about your dreams. They are dream killers and you should not be listened to them. You can have my permission to dream, think, accomplish and achieve all that you can imagine.

REFLECTION

_____

_____

_____

Day 73

I will achieve what I set my mind to achieve.

Your mind is a source of power. The power of positive thinking overcomes the biggest of obstacles. You will achieve exactly on which you set your mind. Try it. Think about nothing and you will achieve nothing. Set it on reading one book each month and you will achieve that. So you can set your mind on whatever you want to achieve and you will do so. Do not underestimate your abilities. There are people who will cross your path who will assist you with your goals as well. Work hard toward your goals. Remove any negative thoughts and all doubt. Your mind directs your actions. Let all of them be positive and all of your energy be directed toward the goal.

REFLECTION

_____

_____

_____

affirmations & advice for girls

Day 74

I am equipped to realize greatness.

You can handle what you have dreamed of and you can reach the goals. There are no conditional statements with that. You must believe that and act accordingly. This is not a dress rehearsal. You need to consider the possibilities of greatness. What does your greatness do for others? What does your greatness do for you? From time to time, I look at what I have accomplish and gasp. That gasp fuels the next achievement. I cannot quit and cannot get discouraged. I have to keep motivated and remain positive. I have to remain focused. I have to remember my charge. I have to remember why I am here. I have to remember my goals. I have to remember that I inspire others. Greatness!

REFLECTION

Day 75

I am amazing!

I am not perfect, but I am amazing!

I want you to say that all day today and every day afterwards. This is not a conceited statement. This is an affirmation. This is not how you feel every day. Some days you will not feel worth a penny. These are words, which will help you to recover from those days. In the meantime, start understanding the measurement of the amazing. You are amazing because you are an overcomer. You are a survivor. You are a positive statistic.

REFLECTION

_____

_____

_____

affirmations & advice for girls

Day 76

I am willing to work hard for what I want.

_____

'If you do not work, then you will not eat.' This statement has been made famous mostly by parents and guardians worldwide when a child becomes grown. However, it bears repeating because your achievement will rest almost entirely on your ability to work hard. Every day. Every night. When you do not feel like it. When you do not have time. When you wish you could talk to or play with your friends. Your hard work and effort are required. This is not a new expectation. You will have to work hard for the rest of your life. The difference is either by force or by choice. At some point, your work will payoff and your efforts will reward you well. Otherwise, you will work hard for others.

REFLECTION

_____
_____
_____

Day 77

My voice is the most important voice I hear.

My voice matters.

Your voice has been at 3 on a scale of 1 to 10. Your voice matters when you are responsible and take action to make changes in your life. This is the best way to get an audience with adults: work and results. As parents and teachers, we want responsible children who become self-sustaining adults. Your voice matters. Speak your truth. Ask for help. Report those who discount your possibilities. Tell someone. If no one responds, call me. I will help you handle it. You are important and so are your words and so is your voice.

REFLECTION

_____

_____

_____

Day 78

My voice has power.

_____

You are the power behind your powerful voice. You have the power to make your voice important. Your voice will have more power if you have knowledge, information and experience. Your voice has power when you achieve your goals, when you make progress in your life, and when you overcome your hurt. Share your voice with others so that they discover the power of their voice. Use this power to propel yourself forward to achievement. Use this power to compel your intrinsic motivation forward. Greatness and power awaits.

REFLECTION

_____
_____
_____

Day 79

I matter!

You are not a mistake! You matter. You are significant. You are rare. You are important. You are kind. You are love. You are healed. You are powerful. You are neat. You are unique. You are special. You are peaceful. You are beautiful. You are amazing.

You are able to do all that you can imagine and think. You are not the statistics they mentioned in that research we read. You are valuable. You are outstanding. You make others consider their accomplishments and you inspire them to pursue their dreams and purpose.

REFLECTION

_____

_____

_____

affirmations & advice for girls

Day 80

I am worthy.

I am worthy of greatness.

No matter what you have been told or think, you are worthy of achieving and accomplishment. You are worthy of being educated and cultured. You are worthy of excellence and leadership. You possess power and intrinsic motivation. You are worthy. You are worthy of greatness. This greatness is not to sit dormant. This requires your action and your attention. You will face opposition in this life. You will meet obstacles. You prove your worth when you decide to overcome.

REFLECTION

_____

_____

_____

Day 81

I am extraordinary.

_____

You are above average. You are beyond ordinary. You are special. You have unique talents and gifts. You have some interesting dreams and goals. You have chosen the road less traveled. You are the solution to so problems, which have yet to exist. You are being groomed to solve them as only you can. Your achievement will set a generation free and on fire to defy all of the odds against them. You are going to redefine 'at-risk.' You are the hope of a whole nation. You are the prize of a community. You are the pride of your family's name. Extraordinary, indeed!

REFLECTION

_____
_____
_____

affirmations & advice for girls

Day 82

I am the example of love.

You did not start out loving but now you are the definition and example of love. You used to hate others and now you love them unconditionally. You would hate but you learned that it requires too much energy, effort and time. You consider the ability to love one of the greatest gifts ever. You share with others how to love and help them to do the same. You value love and you empower others to love themselves and others. You are free and lifted because of love. You have forgiven many so that you can love at the highest possible level. You consider love the fuel you need to reach the next love. You are the example of love others need to give themselves permission to love.

REFLECTION

_____

_____

_____

Day 83

I inspire others to achieve just because I show up.

I will continue to show up.

In the movie, 'Hardball,' the coach tells his team, 'I just admire your ability to show up.' This makes all of the difference. This is the key to success: showing up. This is the key to success. You cannot achieve anything if you do not show up. Perfect attendance at school. Perfect record for turning in assignments. Perfect effort on every test and with every project. Perfect attitude. Perfect respect for adults and fellow students. Perfect respect for property. Showing up is the hardest part. Just show up.

REFLECTION

_____

_____

_____

Day 84

I have a unique and interesting mind: my thoughts are important and intuitive.

I have a unique mind and I know that having a unique mind is sometimes intimidating to others. You need to consider what you are supposed to be doing with that mind, other than worrying about what others think about what you and your thoughts. We have to be concerned with effecting the world and those details, which concern us. We also need to consider how to keep the iron sharp. Read. Study. Research. Collaborate. Partner. We need to consider how to use our mind to change the world for the better and for those who need our help with making those changes.

REFLECTION

Day 85

I am a profound and intricate creation, and I can only be understood with my consent.

Well, this is part of building your self-esteem. You are profound. You are an intricate creation. You can only be understood with your consent. This is hard for some people. You are working to make an impact on the world. This needs to be done with a certain amount of grace and perseverance. Do you like yourself? What does it take to like yourself? Do you love yourself? What does it take to love yourself? What does it take become this person? What does it take to love others?

REFLECTION

_____

_____

_____

affirmations & advice for girls

Day 86

I am great enough as is—no changes are required!

I want you to accept yourself as you are: As Is! You are enough. This is the hardest thing to do. Everyone is going to attempt to change you or enhance you. This may not work or feel natural. You are okay as is. You do not need to change a thing to be a better person. Be okay with who you are. If you do not like a character trait, then consider changing it. But only change it for yourself, not for anyone else. You are a great person as is. No matter what anyone says. I want the best for you. I want you to be your best you. You are enough!

REFLECTION

_____

_____

_____

Day 87

I am worth celebrating!

_____

Did you do well on your report card? Did you do well on your test? How do you celebrate your birthday? How do you like to share good news? How do you want to celebrate major accomplishments? What do you do to have fun? You are worth celebrating. You need to understand how to properly celebrate yourself and others. Celebrate!

REFLECTION

_____
_____
_____

Day 88

I am special.

_____

I am special. I think that you are special too. Other people should think so as well. You should behave in a manner, which influences others to understand that you are special too.

REFLECTION

_____
_____
_____

Day 89

While I appreciate compliments, I do not need them to support or verify my worth.

Worth is defined and developed in two ways. One is how you define your worth. The other is how others define your worth. Those two definitions are developed differently and are based on differing criteria. You develop your definition because of what you think worth is and how you measure up to that definition. Other people will define worth by their personal definition and then they will determine how you measure up to their expectations. This is a horrible measure of worth. You are valuable, regardless of the definition used. Worth is based on self-esteem. Worth is generated by contribution.

REFLECTION

_____

_____

_____

affirmations & advice for girls

Day 90

My success and my desires, my personality, and my activities cause others to be able to be themselves as well.

I think the most important place that people should feel comfortable is within themselves. You should be able to be your authentic self daily. Be yourself. Be your authentic self. Sometimes that authenticity will cause you to make others uncomfortable, but no worries, because at some point your authenticity will cause others to do the same. You are a great person. If there are characteristics or traits, which are not great, then initiate that change. The best gift you can give is to help others understand themselves the way you understand yourself. Be a GREAT you!

REFLECTION

_____

_____

_____

Day 91

My ability to be myself empowers others to do the same.

Someone told me once that I was the most authentic person that he knew. That empowered him and others to do the same. The refreshing part of authenticity is that you never have to remember certain things and you do not have to be uncomfortable ever. Be yourself. Get to know who that is and what that means. Other people are searching for themselves. Help them by being you! It is powerful to be yourself full-time.

REFLECTION

_____

_____

_____

affirmations & advice for girls

Day 92

I am.

_____

Yes, you are. Be comfortable right there. You are enough!

REFLECTION

_____
_____
_____

Day 93

If I respect myself, then others will respect me.

Respect is vague and subjective, neither standard nor consistently defined. What we know for sure is while we do not what respect comprehensively is, we do know for sure what it is not. Do not do things, which would permit someone to be disrespectful.

REFLECTION

_____

_____

_____

Day 94

My excellence will be the new standard.

In a world where the generations are named specifically because of indifference and laziness, this excellence is important as the new standard. This is admirable. I am proud of your stance.

REFLECTION

_____
_____
_____

Day 95

The future I have ahead of me cannot afford for me to quit.

There ain't no quit in me!

I personally cannot quit either. You depend on my sharing my gifts so that you can be inspired and encouraged. I have to keep my word. I have to lead by example. My future does not allow me to quit. Neither does yours. Your future is important. Give it all that you have and then some.

REFLECTION

_____

_____

_____

affirmations & advice for girls

Day 96

I was born to produce!

You are going to produce something. Hopefully, to produce the positive out of life. You were born to produce greatness. You were born to overcome. You were born to be an achiever.

REFLECTION

_____
_____
_____

# 90 Days of Powerful Words

Day 97

I am bold.

I am not going to be afraid of what I have to do. I will move forward with excellence and boldness. I hope that you will do the same. Be Bold!

REFLECTION

_____
_____
_____

affirmations & advice for girls

Day 98

I am brilliant.

One of the things we have to understand is our level. We are brilliant. We work to prove it to ourselves daily. Will we make mistakes? Sure. Part of our brilliance is to understand that we are not perfect. Be brilliant!

REFLECTION

_____

_____

_____

90 Days of Powerful Words

Day 99

I will ask questions so that I can gain clarity about what I do not know.

The only thing I cannot respect is persons who need help but will not ask. Please ask. Get answers. Do not think that you will look less foolish by not asking than to ask for clarity. Nothing is more telling about your knowledge or lack thereof when you make an error and you could have asked and avoided the entire mistake.

REFLECTION

_____

_____

_____

affirmations & advice for girls

Day 100

I am a girl!

I am a girl with a purpose!

I am a girl with a purpose and a message!

_____

I am proud to be a girl. I hope that you are too! You have undiscovered power in being a girl! Use wisely outrageously, and outlandishly!

REFLECTION

_____
_____
_____

90 Days of Powerful Words

affirmations & advice for girls

a final note:

You have come to the end of this affirmation; however you should focus on one for each week going forward. You have a long road and great work ahead, each day is different and has trouble of its very own.

I am impressed with your ability to show up. I have faith that you will use what you already have along with new knowledge and wisdom to achieve and accomplish all that you desire. And help others to do the same.

Learn how to respond to the word no. Learn to be more creative about reaching a yes. Learn to be more creative about getting past the actual obstacle. Keep your composure during all adversity. Think about the consequence for every decision, making that decision judiciously understanding the costs and benefits.

Remember you are not alone. Remember that tragedy is not the end of your story. Remember that you are not a negative statistic.

Hold up your head, especially when you do not feel like it. You cannot see your future with your head down.

Loving yourself is very powerful. I give you permission to do from now until the end of your days. Loving yourself means that you accept you for you are and you comfortable with yourself.

affirmations & advice for girls

In some cultures, girls do not have a voice, are ignored, are treated as if they are sub-citizens, and are outcast for being smart. You are not in the margins of this world. If that is your story, then I empower you to shake off that ideal and embrace the power with which you were born. You are smart. You are whole. You matter. Your opinion is valuable. Your intelligence makes a difference. You have my permission to be smart and study to be an intellectual beast.

I love you and want the very best for you. You have been hurting for so long. Forgive yourself and others no matter how difficult the task. Forgiveness will free from the bondage of that issue and allow you to live again.

The girl in the swing represents who you were and who you want to be. She was fearless! She was bold! She was outlandish! She took the risk to swing. Then she jumped out! You can be her again! Do it!

Go forward and conquer! Do it Big! Do it Afraid! Do it Now!

Love in purple!

From another girl who can identify with you,

Onedia N. Gage

Clear the Mechanism

By Onedia N. Gage, Ph. D.

Quiet so I CAN focus
Stop speaking negative thoughts into my being

QUIET so I can focus
Stop delivering the negative you hope I adopt

Quiet so I can FOCUS
Stop filling me with stuff that falters my progress

Quiet so I can focus
Stop calling me out of my name

CLEAR the mechanism
Clear THE mechanism
Clear the MECHANISM

Clear my mind for the "stuff" that
    Needs my focus

Clear my heart for the "stuff" that
    Requires my attention

Clear my soul for the "stuff" that
    Qualities for commitment

CLEAR the mechanism

Clear THE mechanism
Clear the MECHANISM

When the world is rambunctious around me
Clear the mechanism

When the world rejects me
Clear the mechanism

When the world reacts negatively to the good I do
Clear the mechanism

While the world is questioning who I am
Clear the mechanism

While the world is asking why I am
Clear the mechanism

When the world is asking why do I do what I do
Clear the mechanism

When the world is asking how I do what I do
Clear the mechanism

Identity Crisis

By Onedia N. Gage, Ph. D.

Her words hit me like cold water
Are you mixed
Are you black
I'm black too
Her identity attached to the shallowest of measures
Yet important, extremely

Searching for an identity match
Same shade
Same smile
Same circumstances
Same passion
Searching for the DNA match

Ordinary enough   to fit in
Unique enough   to raise an eyebrow
Distinct enough   to be set apart

No mother near
Mother figure distant in generations
Distant still in relationship

Consistently searching for answers
Countless searches for feedback
Command attention by any means necessary

affirmations & advice for girls

Just a little time
Answers to questions
From a wondering mind
From a lonely heart

Just some attention
From the right person
Would propel her forward

Don't shed another tear
You will succeed
Just a little help you need

Quit checking for the identity
In ordinary things
Rather start inside

> The identity is in her eyes.

Reprinted from <u>In Purple Ink: Poetry for the Spirit</u>

The Nerve to Dream

By Onedia N. Gage, Ph. D.

You have the nerve to dream
And expect others to do the same
The audacity

You know dreams don't come true
You know that we don't leave our circumstances
You know that we cannot convince others to believe falsely

You have the nerve and the audacity
To expect us to dream
When there is blight and slums and
Economic hardships

You still dream for better than we have it
Better than <u>all</u> our ancestors
We have more educated
We have more educators
We have more leaders
We have more politicians
We have more wealthy
We have more
. . . yet you still dream of more

You dream that still more can happen
The audacity of you
And the nerve

And the gall of
You to tell our children that they
Can have more than we have
Define more
How much more
More with what?
Less?

Dreams.
You still do it
And in the worst of times
By perception
By the naked eye
But up close they deserve every opportunity to dream
They deserve hopes
They deserve dreams
They deserve the audacity to look at me and
<u>Know</u> that they too can have what we have
And have more of it.

You still dream.

Reprinted from <u>In Purple Ink: Poetry for the Spirit</u>

90 Days of Powerful Words

resources

www.agirlsday.org

www.mymotherdaughter.com

www.onediagagespeaks.com

www.girlsinc.org

www.haul.org

Love Languages for Teens by Gary Chapman

affirmations & advice for girls

acknowledgments

God, thank You for Your plans for me. Thank You for ***90 Days of Powerful Words: Affirmations and Advice*** and choosing me to complete Your project. I just want to please You. Thank You for continuing to anoint me and to invest in me and my gifts, which keep surprising me. Thank You for loving and forgiving me.

Hillary and Nehemiah, thank you for supporting me and my endeavors. Thank you for loving me, especially when I do nothing without a pen and a clipboard, thank you for enduring my late nights, your ideas, the sounding board, the love and the support. Thank you for celebrating our legacy.

To the girls who have raised their hands in need of these affirmations. I don't know all of you, but to the ones I do know, I apologize. I got it to you as quickly as I could. I love you!

To my prayer partners and to my accountability partners, thank you for the long talks and the powerful prayers and the encouragement. To my pastor and church family, thank you so much for your love and support.

affirmations & advice for girls

Onedia N. Gage, Ph. D., seeks to share her outlandish pursuit of education and value for girls with all who need to enhance her self-esteem. Please seek your authentic self. Gage is a true advocate for all girls. As a girl who had a few advocates, she still could have used more. Still needs one now.

Please feel free to contact her.
onediagage@onediagagespeaks.com, or @onediangage (twitter). www.onediagagespeaks.com

Blogtalkradio.com/onediagage

Youtube.com/onediagage10

Facebook.com/onedia-gage

affirmations & advice for girls

ADVOCATE ♦ TEACHER ♦ FACILITATOR

CONFERENCE SPEAKER ♦ WORKSHOP LEADER

To invite Dr. Onedia Gage to speak to the teens at your school or organization,

Please contact us at: www.onediagagespeaks.com

@onediangage (twitter) ♦ onediagage@onediagagespeaks.com
♦ facebook.com/onediagage
youtube.com/onediagage10 ♦ blogtalkradio.com/onediagage ♦ ongage (Instagram)

affirmations & advice for girls

90 Days of Powerful Words

Publishing

Do you have a book you want to write, but do not know what to do?
Do you have a book you need to publish but do not know how to start?
Would publishing move your career forward?

Let us help

onediagage@purpleink.net ♦ www.purpleink.net

281.740.5143 ♦ 512.715.4243

www.ingramcontent.com/pod-product-compliance
Lightning Source LLC
Chambersburg PA
CBHW070053120526
44588CB00033B/1418